Novena to St Veronica Giuliani:

The powerful meditation and devotion prayer book

Esther J. Haynes

Table of Content

Introduction to St Veronica Giuliani Novena

In the Catholic tradition, novenas are a form of prayer that involves praying for nine consecutive days with the specific intention of seeking the intercession of a particular saint. Novenas provides an opportunity for us to deepen our faith, grow in holiness, and seek the intercession of the saints who have gone before us.

One such saint whose intercession we seek is St. Veronica Giuliani. Born in Italy in 1660, St. Veronica was a Capuchin Poor Clare nun known for her mystical experiences and profound holiness. She dedicated her life to prayer, penance, and serving the poor and the sick. St. Veronica received the stigmata, the wounds of Christ, which she bore with great humility and love.

St. Veronica Giuliani serves as a model of faith, compassion, humility, and surrender to God's will. Her life teaches us the importance of prayer, selfless love, and deep trust in God's providence. Through her example, she inspires us to live more fully in union with God and to imitate the virtues she so beautifully embodied.

During this novena, we will reflect upon different aspects of St. Veronica's life and seek her intercession for specific intentions. Each day will include prayers, reflections, and scripture readings that will help us draw closer to God and embrace the virtues exemplified by St. Veronica Giuliani.

As we embark on this novena, let us open our hearts to the graces and blessings that God wishes to bestow upon us through the intercession of St. Veronica Giuliani. May this time of prayer and reflection deepen our faith, inspire us to greater acts of love and charity, and draw us into a closer relationship with our Heavenly Father.

Let us begin this novena with faith and trust, confident that through the intercession of St. Veronica Giuliani, our prayers will be heard and answered according to God's loving will.

Who is St Veronica Giuliani

St. Veronica Giuliani, born Orsola Giuliani in Italy in 1660, was a devout Catholic nun who lived a life of deep holiness and spiritual intimacy with God. She entered the Capuchin Poor Clares convent at the age of 17 and embraced a life of poverty, prayer, and penance.

St. Veronica experienced numerous mystical phenomena, including visions, ecstasies, and the receiving of the stigmata, the wounds of Christ. Despite her extraordinary spiritual experiences, she remained humble and obedient, always seeking to live by God's will.

Known for her selfless love and compassion, St. Veronica dedicated herself to serving the poor and the sick. She saw the face of Christ in those who were suffering and reached out to them with kindness and care. St. Veronica's life teaches us the importance of charity, humility, and surrendering ourselves completely to God.

Her spiritual insights and writings have had a profound impact on the spiritual life of many. St. Veronica Giuliani was canonized as a saint by Pope Gregory XVI in 1839, recognizing her extraordinary sanctity and the enduring relevance of her teachings.

Today, St. Veronica Giuliani is venerated as the patron saint of the Adoration of the Blessed Sacrament and of those suffering from illnesses. Many seek her intercession for healing, spiritual growth, and guidance in their spiritual journeys.

Through the St. Veronica Giuliani Novena, we have the opportunity to learn from her example, seek her intercession, and draw closer to God. May her life and teachings continue to inspire us to live lives of faith, compassion, and deep union with our Heavenly Father.

The importance of St Veronica Giuliani Novena

The St. Veronica Giuliani Novena holds great importance for those who seek spiritual growth, guidance, and the intercession of St. Veronica Giuliani. Here are a few reasons why this novena is significant:

1. Deepening our faith: The novena provides a structured and focused period of prayer and reflection, allowing us to deepen our faith and strengthen our relationship with God. Through the intercession of St. Veronica Giuliani, we can seek a closer union with Him and grow in our understanding of His love and mercy.

2. Seeking intercession: Novenas are a powerful way to seek the intercession of the saints. St. Veronica Giuliani, known for her holiness and union with God, can serve as a powerful advocate on our behalf. By praying this novena, we place

our intentions and needs before her, trusting in her intercession and the graces that flow from it.

3. Embracing virtues: Each day of the novena focuses on different virtues and aspects of St. Veronica Giuliani's life, such as humility, faith, love, and surrender to God's will. By reflecting on her example and striving to imitate these virtues, we can grow in holiness and become more Christ-like in our own lives.

4. Inspiration from a holy life: St. Veronica Giuliani's life and teachings continue to inspire countless people. Her dedication to prayer, selfless love, and humility serve as a model for us to follow. The novena allows us to learn from her example and apply her insights to our spiritual journeys.

5. Encountering God's grace: Engaging in the St. Veronica Giuliani Novena opens us

to the receiver's abundant grace. As we pray and reflect, we create space within ourselves for God to work and transform us. By seeking St. Veronica's intercession, we invite the power of God's love and mercy into our lives.

Overall, the St. Veronica Giuliani Novena provides an opportunity to deepen our faith, seek the intercession of a holy saint, and grow in virtue. Through this focused period of prayer and reflection, we open ourselves to the transformative power of God's grace and draw closer to Him, guided by the example of St. Veronica Giuliani.

Day 1

Opening Prayer:
In the name of the Father, and of the Son, and the Holy Spirit. Amen.

Heavenly Father, we gather here today to begin this novena in honor of St. Veronica Giuliani. We thank you for the gift of her holy life and her example of selfless love for you. As we embark on this novena, we ask for her intercession and guidance. Help us to grow closer to you and to follow the path of holiness, just as she did. May her virtues inspire us and her prayers strengthen us. We pray this in the name of Jesus Christ, your Son, who lives and reigns with you and the Holy Spirit, one God, forever and ever. Amen.

Reflection:
Today, let us reflect upon the life of St. Veronica Giuliani and her deep love for Jesus. She was a Capuchin Poor Clare nun who lived in Italy in the 17th century. From a young age, she desired to dedicate her life to Christ, and at the age of

17, she entered the convent. Throughout her life, St. Veronica experienced intense mystical experiences and received the stigmata, the wounds of Christ, on her body.

St. Veronica embraced suffering and offered it as a sacrifice for the salvation of souls. Her life was marked by humility, obedience, and a profound union with God. She wrote numerous spiritual writings that continue to inspire and guide people in their journey toward God. Today, we seek her intercession and ask for her help in deepening our love for Jesus and our willingness to embrace the crosses in our lives.

Scripture Reading:
"Whoever does not take up their cross and follow me is not worthy of me." (Matthew 10:38)

Prayer to St. Veronica Giuliani:
O St. Veronica Giuliani, you who embraced the cross of Christ with great love and devotion, we turn to you in this novena seeking your

intercession. Help us to carry our crosses with courage and trust in God's providence. Teach us to surrender our will to God's will and to offer our sufferings for the salvation of souls. Pray for us, dear St. Veronica, that we may grow in holiness and draw closer to Jesus, who lives and reigns with the Father and the Holy Spirit, one God, forever and ever. Amen.

Concluding Prayer:

Heavenly Father, we thank you for the graces we have received on this first day of the novena. May the example of St. Veronica Giuliani inspire us to love you more deeply and to embrace the crosses in our lives with faith and trust. Grant us the strength to follow your will and the courage to imitate the virtues of your holy servant. We ask this through Christ our Lord. Amen.

May the blessings of Almighty God, the Father, Son, and Holy Spirit, descend upon us and remain with us always. Amen.

Day 2

Opening Prayer:
In the name of the Father, and of the Son, and the Holy Spirit. Amen.

Heavenly Father, we come before you on this second day of the novena, seeking the intercession of St. Veronica Giuliani. Help us to learn from her example of fidelity and perseverance in following you. As we reflect on her life today, may her virtues inspire us and her prayers guide us. We ask for the grace to imitate her deep love for Jesus and her unwavering commitment to your will. We pray this in the name of Jesus Christ, your Son, who lives and reigns with you and the Holy Spirit, one God, forever and ever. Amen.

Reflection:
Today, let us reflect upon the virtue of humility, which was one of the defining characteristics of St. Veronica Giuliani's life. Despite her numerous mystical experiences and the spiritual

gifts she received, she remained humble and saw herself as a lowly servant of God. St. Veronica recognized that all the good in her came from God, and she attributed everything to His grace.

Her humility allowed her to be open to God's will and to accept whatever came her way with gratitude. She saw herself as nothing and desired only to serve God and her community with great love. St. Veronica teaches us that true greatness lies in humble service and in recognizing our dependence on God.

Scripture Reading:
"Humble yourselves before the Lord, and he will lift you." (James 4:10)

Prayer to St. Veronica Giuliani:
O St. Veronica Giuliani, you who lived a life of profound humility, we seek your intercession on this second day of the novena. Help us to embrace the virtue of humility and to recognize our dependence on God's grace. Teach us to serve others with love and to seek the glory of

God above all else. Pray for us, dear St. Veronica, that we may grow in humility and become true witnesses of Christ's love in the world. We ask this through Christ our Lord. Amen.

Concluding Prayer:
Heavenly Father, we thank you for the graces we have received on this second day of the novena. May the example of St. Veronica Giuliani inspire us to embrace humility and to serve you and others with love. Grant us the grace to imitate her humble spirit and to recognize our dependence on you in all things. We ask this through Christ our Lord. Amen.

May the blessings of Almighty God, the Father, Son, and Holy Spirit, descend upon us and remain with us always. Amen.

Day 3

Opening Prayer:
In the name of the Father, and of the Son, and the Holy Spirit. Amen.

Heavenly Father, on this third day of the novena, we gather to seek the intercession of St. Veronica Giuliani. Help us to learn from her life of prayer and union with you. As we reflect on her example today, may her deep love for the Eucharist inspire us to grow in our devotion to this great sacrament. Grant us the grace to approach the Eucharist with reverence and gratitude. We pray this in the name of Jesus Christ, your Son, who lives and reigns with you and the Holy Spirit, one God, forever and ever. Amen.

Reflection:
St. Veronica Giuliani had a profound love for the Eucharist, which she considered the source and summit of her spiritual life. She recognized the real presence of Jesus in the Blessed Sacrament

and spent hours in adoration, pouring out her love and adoration before the Lord. St. Veronica teaches us the importance of deepening our relationship with Jesus through regular participation in the Eucharist and spending time in his presence.

Just as St. Veronica found solace, strength, and nourishment in the Eucharist, we too can experience the transforming power of Christ's body and blood in our lives. The Eucharist unites us with Christ and strengthens our union with him. Through the Eucharist, we are nourished and empowered to live as faithful disciples.

Scripture Reading:
"I am the living bread that came down from heaven. Whoever eats of this bread will live forever, and the bread that I will give for the life of the world is my flesh." (John 6:51)

Prayer to St. Veronica Giuliani:
O St. Veronica Giuliani, you who had a deep love and devotion for the Eucharist, we seek

your intercession on this third day of the novena. Help us to approach the Eucharist with reverence and awe, recognizing the true presence of Jesus in this sacred sacrament. May our participation in the Eucharist transform us and deepen our union with Christ. Pray for us, dear St. Veronica, that we may always hunger for the Bread of Life and find our nourishment and strength in the Eucharist. We ask this through Christ our Lord. Amen.

Concluding Prayer:
Heavenly Father, we thank you for the graces we have received on this third day of the novena. May the example of St. Veronica Giuliani inspire us to deepen our love and devotion for the Eucharist. Grant us the grace to approach this sacred sacrament with reverence and gratitude, and to be transformed by our encounter with Jesus. We ask this through Christ our Lord. Amen.

May the blessings of Almighty God, the Father, Son, and Holy Spirit, descend upon us and remain with us always. Amen.

Day 4

Opening Prayer:
In the name of the Father, and of the Son, and the Holy Spirit. Amen.

Heavenly Father, on this fourth day of the novena, we come before you seeking the intercession of St. Veronica Giuliani. Help us to learn from her life of penance and self-denial. As we reflect on her example today, may her spirit of sacrifice inspire us to offer our lives as a pleasing sacrifice to you. Grant us the grace to embrace penance and self-discipline for the sake of our spiritual growth. We pray this in the name of Jesus Christ, your Son, who lives and reigns with you and the Holy Spirit, one God, forever and ever. Amen.

Reflection:
St. Veronica Giuliani embraced a life of penance and self-denial as a means of drawing closer to God and offering reparation for sin. She willingly embraced the crosses and sufferings

that came her way, recognizing them as opportunities for purification and spiritual growth. St. Veronica teaches us the importance of self-discipline and the willingness to sacrifice for the sake of the Kingdom of God.

In our own lives, we are called to imitate her example by embracing penance and self-denial. This may involve acts of fasting, prayer, almsgiving, or other forms of self-sacrifice. By offering these acts with a spirit of love and surrender, we can unite ourselves more closely to Christ and participate in his redemptive work.

Scripture Reading:
"Then Jesus told his disciples, 'If any want to become my followers, let them deny themselves and take up their cross and follow me.'"
(Matthew 16:24)

Prayer to St. Veronica Giuliani:
O St. Veronica Giuliani, you who embraced a life of penance and self-denial for the love of God, we seek your intercession on this fourth

day of the novena. Help us to imitate your spirit of sacrifice and to embrace self-discipline for the sake of our spiritual growth. Grant us the grace to offer our lives as a pleasing sacrifice to God and to unite our sufferings with those of Jesus. Pray for us, dear St. Veronica, that we may learn to deny ourselves and follow Christ more faithfully. We ask this through Christ our Lord. Amen.

Concluding Prayer:
Heavenly Father, we thank you for the graces we have received on this fourth day of the novena. May the example of St. Veronica Giuliani inspire us to embrace penance and self-denial as means of growing closer to you. Grant us the grace to willingly carry our crosses and to offer our lives as a pleasing sacrifice to you. We ask this through Christ our Lord. Amen.

May the blessings of Almighty God, the Father, Son, and Holy Spirit, descend upon us and remain with us always. Amen.

Day 5

Opening Prayer:

In the name of the Father, and of the Son, and the Holy Spirit. Amen.

Heavenly Father, as we embark on the fifth day of this novena, we turn to you with hearts full of gratitude for the gift of St. Veronica Giuliani. Help us to learn from her life of obedience and trust in your divine will. As we reflect on her example today, may her unwavering obedience inspire us to submit our own will to yours. Grant us the grace to trust in your providence and to embrace your plans for our lives. We pray this in the name of Jesus Christ, your Son, who lives and reigns with you and the Holy Spirit, one God, forever and ever. Amen.

Reflection:

St. Veronica Giuliani exemplified obedience throughout her life. She had a deep desire to align her will with the will of God and to fulfill his plans for her. Even in the face of great challenges and difficulties, she remained obedient and submitted herself to the guidance of her superiors and the teachings of the Church. St. Veronica teaches us that obedience is an act of trust and surrender to God, recognizing that he knows what is best for us.

In our own lives, we are called to imitate her example of obedience. This includes obedience to God's commandments, the teachings of the Church, and the authorities placed over us. Through obedience, we grow in humility and allow God to lead us on the path of holiness.

Scripture Reading:
"Jesus answered them, 'My teaching is not mine but his who sent me.'" (John 7:16)

Prayer to St. Veronica Giuliani:
O St. Veronica Giuliani, you who embraced obedience as a way of aligning your will with God's divine plan, we seek your intercession on this fifth day of the novena. Help us to imitate your obedience and to trust in God's providential

care. Grant us the grace to submit our will to the will of God, even when it is difficult or challenging. Pray for us, dear St. Veronica, that we may grow in obedience and trust in God's loving guidance. We ask this through Christ our Lord. Amen.

Concluding Prayer:

Heavenly Father, we thank you for the graces we have received on this fifth day of the novena. May the example of St. Veronica Giuliani inspire us to embrace obedience and trust in your divine will. Grant us the grace to align our will with yours and to trust in your providential care for us. We ask this through Christ our Lord. Amen.

May the blessings of Almighty God, the Father, Son, and Holy Spirit, descend upon us and remain with us always. Amen.

Day 6

Opening Prayer:

In the name of the Father, and of the Son, and the Holy Spirit. Amen.

Heavenly Father, on this sixth day of the novena, we come before you seeking the intercession of St. Veronica Giuliani. Help us to learn from her life of compassion and love for the poor and the suffering. As we reflect on her example today, may her selfless acts of charity inspire us to reach out to those in need. Grant us the grace to be instruments of your love and mercy in the world. We pray this in the name of Jesus Christ, your Son, who lives and reigns with you and the Holy Spirit, one God, forever and ever. Amen.

Reflection:

St. Veronica Giuliani had a compassionate heart, and she dedicated herself to serving the poor and the suffering. She saw the face of Christ in those who were in need and reached out to them with love and care. St. Veronica teaches us that charity is not merely a duty but a response to the love and mercy we have received from God. Through acts of selfless love and compassion, we can be channels of God's grace and bring comfort to those who are hurting.

In our own lives, we are called to imitate her example of charity. We are called to see the needs of others, to offer our help and support, and to share what we have with those who are less fortunate. By reaching out to the poor, the sick, and the marginalized, we can bring hope and healing to their lives.

Scripture Reading:
"Truly I tell you, just as you did it to one of the least of these who are members of my family, you did it to me." (Matthew 25:40)

Prayer to St. Veronica Giuliani:
O St. Veronica Giuliani, you who had a compassionate heart and reached out to the poor and the suffering, we seek your intercession on this sixth day of the novena. Help us to imitate

your selfless love and to see the face of Christ in those who are in need. Grant us the grace to be instruments of your compassion and mercy, bringing comfort and hope to those who are hurting. Pray for us, dear St. Veronica, that we may extend our love and care to all our brothers and sisters. We ask this through Christ our Lord. Amen.

Concluding Prayer:
Heavenly Father, we thank you for the graces we have received on this sixth day of the novena. May the example of St. Veronica Giuliani inspire us to practice charity and compassion towards those in need. Grant us the grace to see the face of Christ in others and to be instruments of your love and mercy. We ask this through Christ our Lord. Amen.

May the blessings of Almighty God, the Father, Son, and Holy Spirit, descend upon us and remain with us always. Amen.

Day 7

Opening Prayer:
In the name of the Father, and of the Son, and the Holy Spirit. Amen.

Heavenly Father, as we gather on this seventh day of the novena, we seek the intercession of St. Veronica Giuliani. Help us to learn from her life of humility and surrender to your divine will. As we reflect on her example today, may her deep humility inspire us to embrace true greatness in your kingdom. Grant us the grace to surrender ourselves completely to you and to humbly serve others in love. We pray this in the name of Jesus Christ, your Son, who lives and reigns with you and the Holy Spirit, one God, forever and ever. Amen.

Reflection:
St. Veronica Giuliani was a model of humility. Despite her many spiritual gifts and mystical experiences, she remained humble, recognizing that everything she had was a gift from God. St.

Veronica teaches us that true greatness lies in humble service and self-emptying love. It is by acknowledging our dependence on God and recognizing the dignity of every person that we can live out the call to humility.

In our own lives, we are called to imitate her example of humility. We are called to embrace a posture of selflessness, putting the needs of others before our own and seeking to serve rather than be served. By cultivating humility, we open ourselves to God's grace and become vessels of his love in the world.

Scripture Reading:
"Whoever becomes humble like this child is the greatest in the kingdom of heaven." (Matthew 18:4)

Prayer to St. Veronica Giuliani:
O St. Veronica Giuliani, you who lived a life of profound humility and surrender to God's will, we seek your intercession on this seventh day of the novena. Help us to imitate your humility and

to recognize that everything we have is a gift from God. Grant us the grace to embrace true greatness by humbly serving others and surrendering ourselves completely to God. Pray for us, dear St. Veronica, that we may grow in humility and love. We ask this through Christ our Lord. Amen.

Concluding Prayer:
Heavenly Father, we thank you for the graces we have received on this seventh day of the novena. May the example of St. Veronica Giuliani inspire us to embrace humility and surrender to your divine will. Grant us the grace to recognize our dependence on you and to serve others with selflessness and love. We ask this through Christ our Lord. Amen.

May the blessings of Almighty God, the Father, Son, and Holy Spirit, descend upon us and remain with us always. Amen.

Day 8

Opening Prayer:

In the name of the Father, and of the Son, and the Holy Spirit. Amen.

Heavenly Father, as we gather on this eighth day of the novena, we seek the intercession of St. Veronica Giuliani. Help us to learn from her life of faith and trust in your providence. As we reflect on her example today, may her unwavering faith inspire us to deepen our trust in you. Grant us the grace to surrender our fears and worries to you and to embrace a childlike faith. We pray this in the name of Jesus Christ, your Son, who lives and reigns with you and the Holy Spirit, one God, forever and ever. Amen.

Reflection:

St. Veronica Giuliani had a profound faith in God's providence. She trusted that God would provide for her needs and guide her on the path of holiness. Despite the challenges and uncertainties she faced, she remained steadfast in her belief that God's love and care were always present. St. Veronica teaches us the importance of entrusting ourselves completely to God and placing our faith in his plans for us.

In our own lives, we are called to imitate her example of faith. We are called to trust in God's providence, even when we face difficulties or uncertainties. By surrendering our fears and worries to him, we open ourselves to the peace and assurance that come from knowing that God is with us every step of the way.

Scripture Reading:
"Now faith is the assurance of things hoped for, the conviction of things not seen." (Hebrews 11:1)

Prayer to St. Veronica Giuliani:
O St. Veronica Giuliani, you who had unwavering faith and trust in God's providence, we seek your intercession on this eighth day of the novena. Help us to imitate your childlike faith and to surrender our worries and fears to

God. Grant us the grace to trust in his loving
care and to believe in his plans for our lives.
Pray for us, dear St. Veronica, that our faith may
deepen and sustain us in all circumstances. We
ask this through Christ our Lord. Amen.

Concluding Prayer:
Heavenly Father, we thank you for the graces we
have received on this eighth day of the novena.
May the example of St. Veronica Giuliani inspire
us to deepen our faith and trust in your
providence. Grant us the grace to surrender our
worries and fears to you and to embrace a
childlike faith in your loving care. We ask this
through Christ our Lord. Amen.

May the blessings of Almighty God, the Father,
Son, and Holy Spirit, descend upon us and
remain with us always. Amen.

Day 9

Opening Prayer:

In the name of the Father, and of the Son, and the Holy Spirit. Amen.

Heavenly Father, as we gather on this ninth and final day of the novena, we seek the intercession of St. Veronica Giuliani. Help us to learn from her life of holiness and union with you. As we reflect on her example today, may her deep spiritual union inspire us to draw closer to you in prayer and contemplation. Grant us the grace to seek You above all else and to live in intimate communion with You. We pray this in the name of Jesus Christ, your Son, who lives and reigns with you and the Holy Spirit, one God, forever and ever. Amen.

Reflection:

St. Veronica Giuliani had a profound spiritual union with God. She dedicated herself to a life of prayer and contemplation, seeking to know and love God intimately. Her heart was always turned towards him, and she found solace and strength in his presence. St. Veronica teaches us the importance of cultivating our relationship with God and seeking him above all else.

In our own lives, we are called to imitate her example of spiritual union. We are called to make prayer and contemplation a priority, carving out moments of silence and solitude to be with God. By seeking him in the stillness of our hearts, we can deepen our intimacy with him and allow his grace to transform us from within.

Scripture Reading:
"But when you pray, go into your room, close the door, and pray to your Father, who is unseen. Then your Father, who sees what is done in secret, will reward you." (Matthew 6:6)

Prayer to St. Veronica Giuliani:
O St. Veronica Giuliani, you who had a deep spiritual union with God and found solace in his presence, we seek your intercession on this ninth and final day of the novena. Help us to imitate

your dedication to prayer and contemplation, and to seek God above all else. Grant us the grace to cultivate a vibrant spiritual life and to live in intimate communion with our Heavenly Father. Pray for us, dear St. Veronica, that we may grow in holiness and draw closer to God each day. We ask this through Christ our Lord. Amen.

Concluding Prayer:
Heavenly Father, we thank you for the graces we have received during this novena, especially on this ninth day. May the example of St. Veronica Giuliani inspire us to deepen our spiritual lives and seek you above all else. Grant us the grace to cultivate a vibrant prayer life and to live in intimate communion with you. We ask this through Christ our Lord. Amen.

May the blessings of Almighty God, the Father, Son, and Holy Spirit, descend upon us and remain with us always. Amen.

Printed in Great Britain
by Amazon

35150558R00030